MONOLOGUE

On the Shores of the River of Life

Alexandra Roceric

 iUniverse®

MONOLOGUE
ON THE SHORES OF THE RIVER OF LIFE

iUniverse books may be ordered through booksellers or by contacting:

iUniverse
1663 Liberty Drive
Bloomington, IN 47403
www.iuniverse.com
1-800-Authors (1-800-288-4677)

ISBN: 978-1-5320-0727-9 (sc)
ISBN: 978-1-5320-0726-2 (e)

Library of Congress Control Number: 2016915524

Print information available on the last page.

iUniverse rev. date: 09/26/2016

[Credits:]

o   Our special friend, James B. Moldovan, a bilingual <u>belles-lettres</u> man, did not only greatly improve the English translation made by the author, but understood profoundly the spirit in which these pages were written.

o   Cover by Ion Manta

To my forever husband
Iliuță (Ilie, Lee) Chioariu,
in loving memory.

I am talking with you
about myself
me, whom
my mind alone
cannot dechiper

I am talking with myself
about you
you, who's been waiting
for a long time
to get a real reflection

You are talking with yourself
you are talking with me
using words to their whole capacity
in words, as well as in silence
you, me: one entity

(Alexandra Roceric)

Monologue on the Shores of the River of Life

Alexandra Roceric

As you open this volume—one proffered by a Romanian-born linguist and poet—you might be tempted to think, "Aha! Another émigrée publication." You could even suspect that *Monologue* springs from the emigrant experience--that relocating from Bucharest to Washington, D.C. might stand at the core of this very personal work. It does not.

Both the linguist and the poet love words and love using them well. Both the linguist and the poet are aware of the transformative power of the word and view this power with some degree of fear. They both love words, they both understand power of the word, and they both struggle to express words—especially in a personal narrative. More critically, they both attempt to make sense of life and to segment life's transformational events precisely **with words.**

For this author that life-changing event was not the move to the "New World," but rather what happened afterwards—specifically meeting my husband, Iliuță (as the Romanian says, "Of eternal memory"). Iliuță changed my life, he transformed my life, he completed my life. The current volume reflects my insights that come as a result of knowing him—happily—for more than 30 years.

I sincerely hope that you enjoy these "words."

—Washington, D.C., Spring, 2016.

Index

D	E	F
Day	Elegance	Face
Death	Embarrassment	Faith
Declaration	Empathy	Fashion
Defeat	Enamored	Fault
Delicacy	Enemy	Fear
Dependence	Envy	Feel
Despair	Equal	Feeling
Destiny	Event	Flaw
Destroy	Exasperation	Forgiveness
Dialogue	Expectation	Friend
Difference		Friendship
Direction		Future
Disappoint		
Discretion		
Disrespect		G
Do		
Do evil		Generosity
Doubt		God
Dream		Good
		Good deed
		Gratitude
		Greed

H

Habit
Happy
Harmony
Hate
Have
Help
Hiding place
Holiday
Hope

I

If
Ignore
Illusion
Imagination
Impatience
Important
Incomplete
Indecisiveness
Indifference
Insult
Intelligent
Interesting
Intimacy
Isolation

J

Joy

K

Keep quiet
Kiss
Know

L

Language
  Foreign language
  Mother language
Laugh
Laziness
Lazy
Learn
Lie
Life
Light
Listen
Live
Loneliness
Longing
Lose
Love

M

Mankind (Man; People)
Memory
Messenger
Middle ground
Mirror
Mistake
Moment
Mother
Music
Mystery

N

Never
Night
Nightmare
Nostalgia
Notable point
Nuance
Numbness

O

Object
Oblivion
Obsession
Old age
Old people
Opinion
Optimism
Original
Originality

P

Passion
Past
Patience
Placidity
Plans
Play
Polyglot
Power
Pray
Prayer
Predestinate
Prefer
Present
Pride
Principle
Project
Promise
Proud
Punishment

Q

Question
Quietude

R

Rape
Reaction
Relationship
Remorse
Renunciation
Repetition
Replace
Reproach
Resignation
Responsibility
Revenge
Rise
Risk
Routine
Rushing

S

Sacrifice
Seasons
Secret
Seem
Self-define
Self-love
Self-portrait
Selfishness
Sense
Sentimentalist
Separation
Shame
Silence
Sin
Sleep
Space
Sphinx
Stubborn
Stubbornness
Suffer
Suffering
Suicide
Surprise
Suspicious

T

Taboo
Talk
Tango
Tear
Technology
Telepathy
Thank you
Therapist
Think
Thought
Time
Tolerance
Trace
Trust
Truth
Try

U

Understand
Understanding
Unhappiness

V

Victim

W

Wait
Waltz
War
Weakness
Will
Wing
Wisdom
Woman
Wonder
Word
   Ugly words

A

- ABANDON

    - To abandon another person is a brutal act. Abandonment attacks without kindness, without generosity. It does not try to soften the sadness that comes of separation.

- ABSENCE

    - Only somebody who is deeply integrated in your universe can leave behind a palpable absence. Otherwise, everything passes …

- ACCIDENTAL

    - When we do not understand the causes, the consequences, the order of things, we conclude that something was "accidental."

- ACT

    - In contrast to why we cannot do something, there is the powerful how to act. So we pass over the doubts, the "if we only were able …"

- ADMIRE

    - One has to be generous in order to be able to admire honestly, to admire joyfully.

- ADVANCE

  - The world advances neither by optimists nor pessimists—but by both. Sometimes their dialog appears to be in conflict.

- ADVICE

  - We are always waiting for our friends' advice in crucial moments. Do they have a right or a duty to advise us?

  - If we only could lead our lives in agreement with the (good) advice we are giving to others!

  - Advice given with the expectation that it must be followed becomes a burden instead of being helpful.

  - Advices about what you should do, whom you should ask for help, where you should place your requests, etc. are so ugly. They reflect their authors' every intention to stay uninvolved. Such people try to replace real participation with so called wise opinions, avoiding efforts and distancing themselves from those in need, and they even expect gratitude for their attitude.

- AGE

  - You can approach age in many ways. But there is no way to dissociate yourself from it.

  - Soul and body do not age in concert. Your body creaks, while your heart rushes with joy—resisting and still exploring. By contrast, a soul stunted by blows ... pants ... tired of its body-house. Obstinately, they join forces—together traversing the final piece of life and proclaiming its end.

- ALLIANCE

    - Needing to feel accepted, validated, approved, applauded, praised, admired – people resort to strange alliances. Occasionally, such relations can even include (potential) enemies.

    - We are bragging about our alliances, but we are dissimulating our complicities.

- ALONE

    - Alone means emptied as well.

    - To live by yourself—alone—means being without a mirror, without a shadow, without an echo— lacking in any fair judge.

- AMASS

    - It may be that we amass things hoping that one day they will help us to remember—and so become a kind of memory-guide.

- ANSWER

    - It is impressive what a large number of complex, remarkable, and touching answers we get—unless they are based on misunderstood questions.

- ARROGANT

    - When judging an arrogant person, be careful not to become equally conceited.

- ASK

    - Ask … ask again … pray … implore. But begging?

- ATTACHMENT

    - Are our attachments to people, places, things, ideas – attempts to replace the <u>terra firma</u> of Paradise Lost?

- ATTENTIVE

    - How attentive is it to be attentive enough? In what correlation with to observe, to understand, to feel? How intensely, and with how much perseverance?

B

- BAD LUCK

  - We can always blame our failures on bad luck.

- BANALITY

  - We accept the banal more than we should, for its comfort, the lukewarm moment it provides us. Isn't the boredom it generates in our lives too big a price?

- BE

  - Inseparable entities: we are what we do, and also what we say (let's not treat lightly the "only words!"), and also what we think (sinning just in our thoughts should be much food for ... thought!).

- BE ABLE

  - Wishing to be able ... But also being able to wish ...

- BEAUTIFUL

  - Luckily, there are so many ways to be beautiful.

  - We are all in quest of the beautiful, but we are not even in an unanimous agreement about what that means.

- BEAUTY

  - Beauty remains mysterious, while attempts to define it go on *ad nauseam*. How come we cannot "clarify" what it is that we like—the things that fascinate us? How different it is with the things we dislike intensely … things that fill us with loathing.

  - Make sure that you keep your appreciation for beauty alive … and while admiring it, also remember to avoid any danger of ridicule!

- BEGINNING

  - Nothing is quite so fresh as a beginning … Sadly, we have to learn—over and over—just how briefly one lasts.

- BORE

  - In how many ways can we get bored?

- BOREDOM

  - What is to be found at the opposite pole of boredom?

  - How short is the path between boredom and sadness.

- BORING

  - How boring everything would become if we would always repeat doing what we are taught to do – with good intentions and with kindness – by our parents, teachers, mentors.

- BOUNDARY

    - Both our successes and our haltings are conditioned by limits. Maybe we could put forth our ideal standards and ask ourselves <u>when, where, how</u>, and especially … <u>why</u>?

- BRUTALITY

    - Brutality is not a form of sincerity, even though the two do intersect occasionally.

C

- CARICATURE

    - Why is it so difficult to recognize ourselves in our caricatures?

- CHANGE

    - It may be more important to understand what makes us different from somebody than to try to change that person.

    - Changes in human relations usually lead to the cry: "You've changed!" Each participant shifts a bit, taking turns, doing it gradually, moving in various directions. The complete picture may alter so much so that the initial structure is destroyed. Whom can we reproach? Who gets the blame for the "emergency" of a new kind of connection— or, ultimately, the destruction ... the absolutely modified structure?

- CHILD

    - The end of innocence: the first mean act of a child.

- CHOOSE

    - The chance we have to choose does not simplify our existence at all, but it gives us the illusion of power.

- CLEAR

  - How clearly could you explain to what extent certain things are unclear to you?

- COINCIDENCE

  - Coincidences hinder logical consequences.

- COMFORT

  - Postponing caressing, postponing the offer of comfort is a risk never to be assumed.

  - Know how to comfort—with no illusions that you also will heal …

- COMMUNICATION

  - Nothing without context! What we are stating while "chatting" does not always represent something we would be ready to express publicly and with great conviction. In chatting, we may still be trying to … organize our thoughts. In speaking publicly, responsibility and gravity of words are involved. This means, very different acts of communication.

  - We expect clear messages from good "communicators," while we often neglect the listener in a nonchalant way. We are ready to repeat those things we thought that we understood without mistake, without question. Sometimes we respond with accusations due to a lack of clarity in the speaker's delivery. Failed communication can trigger serious consequences, since patience—the element which supposedly insures mutual understanding—is missing.

- COMPARISON

    - Comparisons help in finding solutions, but they do not suffice for substituting them.

- COMPETITION

    - The spirit of competition is always alive. Competitions attract both future winners and future losers. But only the winners enjoy the victory! And the best seems to be to make a competition between you and yourself and to win it!

- COMPROMISE

    - Compromises consume patience. What they proffer as "solutions," they lack in exuberance.

- CONNECT

    - Memories and future plans are what connects us with people.

- CONTAGIOUS

    - Both intelligence and stupidity are contagious.

- CONTEMPT

  - What entitles us to contempt? Sometimes one is even talking about a "cold contempt". Does our attitude include as much distancing as we pretend?

- CONTINUITY

  - Newness is diluted when we lose a sense of continuity. Continuity moves us through memory, witnesses, echoes, trances, messengers, testaments- -and especially through discreet inspiration.

- CONTRETEMPS

  - Too much sorrow flows from contretemps.

- COSMETIC

  - Cosmetic surgery succeeds in achieving just one kind of performance: it promotes uniformity. It replaces flaws—real or imagined—with features considered beautiful. It is all about standardizing ...

- COWARD

  - It is cowardly to hurt somebody when she/he is most vulnerable. It is something we condemn all too little. Children, the sick, seniors are all good examples of the vulnerable—and make good targets! Cowards are not afraid to face weakness.

  - Cowardice does not represent a deliberate act. The coward reacts according to his own nature, or because he/she did not learn what courage means.

His/her activities mean for him/her the simple price for saving one's own existence.

- CRY

  - My heart—now turned to stone—thanks you for helping me to cry!

- CURIOSITY

  - We discipline our curiosity when we realize that there are answers which we fear.

D

- DAY

  - How many days in your life would you like repeated? How many days would you like to last longer than night?

  - The day named "tomorrow" will soon be called "yesterday."

- DEATH

  - With each death you discover just how difficult the end is. Each way opens other ways towards fear. No death can cure you of the fear of death.

  - Trying to soothe the suffering that comes with death, we habitually and philosophically talk about "celebrating the life" of the deceased. Asymmetrically with the birth of children, no one philosophizes about death—which marks the inevitable end of all lives.

  - Death does not change "some things" in the lives of the mourners left behind to grieve and to remember. Death changes everything and forever.

  - With birth begins the journey towards death. Still, we remain so afraid of it!

- DECLARATION

    - Out-of-place love declarations from a man sound ridiculous; those from a woman seem pathetic. They represent a traditional plot—one in an involuntary show. They are offered with sadness and are received with little tolerance.

- DEFEAT

    - But there are also sublime defeats—more noble, more magnificent, greater, and—especially—more memorable than victories.

- DELICACY

    - We can never be too delicate with someone.

    - One can always reproach another person for a lack of good manners—lacking the politeness acquired by a "code." However, this does not include refinement, delicacy, subtle politeness—which only come via osmosis. Yes, "born finesse" starts at conception.

    - How much delicacy is, indeed, part of real strength!

- DEPENDENCE

    - Is it possible to be good without loving? What about loving without being good? Dependencies?

- DESPAIR

    - When reaching the limit of despair, there is no more room for producing useless words, and only one cry is being heard: "Have mercy, o God, have mercy" (Psalm 57:1).

– Despair explains acts committed without dignity, without honor; however, it can never justify them.

– Despair does not live on a hilltop. It clings to in the crevices below that devour you on your climb upwards.

– The road to despair passes through doubt.

• DESTINY

– Either by science or the occult manner, we are trying to discover what is "unique" about us. The lines in our palm, our face, our fingerprints, a gesture, and now, the DNA – of each of us, are speaking about us. Should we read in these elements, signs of our destinies as well?

– It is fascinating just to watch how and where the arms of destiny will unfold. Destiny pushes boundaries.

– Destiny is so overwhelming, and it displays so many faces. Sometimes we cannot even recognize the hand it extends to manipulate us, and, so, we invent all kinds of explanations …

• DESTROY

– It is amazing what efforts it takes and how much time is invested when we build something, while destruction takes so little time! Fortresses, pyramids, skyscrapers, high walls, towers, palaces, roads above and under the ground are falling ... And how little needs to take place or to be said in order to destroy human relations which appeared to be indestructible, in which whole lives were invested sometimes ...

- DIALOGUE

  - Dialogue becomes suggestive when appositions, parentheses, and paraphrases begin to accumulate. From a distance (maybe so far away as to be unseen), information is offered with politeness and generosity. Increasing clarifications get you to [re] enter a circle that unravels at a certain point ...

- DIFFERENCE

  - There are simply not enough numbers to quantify the differences between us; there probably will never be. Still the inherent, growing brutalization that follows may preclude us from even noticing our differences.

  - To be, to do, to have: "auxiliary" verbs which lead us, they define us predominantly, and they reflect the differences between us.

  - Small differences between people can create situations which are more difficult to reconcile than features which oppose them to each other very clearly, precisely because they are so subtle.

- DIRECTION

    - We cannot take any direction before first determining the point zero. At that moment we need absolute calm. It is also the moment when finding it is most difficult.

- DISAPPOINT

    - Is self-respect a weapon? An armor? All we do points to our desire not to disappoint ourselves. If we don't succeed otherwise, we try to deceive ourselves, or we manage to forget. Unfortunately, not many people are fighting regrets, and fewer yet know what guilty feelings are.

- DISCRETION

    - One should try to avoid mistaking discretion for an obsessive secretiveness, favored by so many weak people. Based on fear, also, maybe.

- DISRESPECT

    - How much disrespect should one tolerate? Absolutely none!

- DO

    - We can do so much—with so little.

- DO EVIL

  - It is never too late to do evil! On the contrary, and any missed "deadline" marks a victory for everybody, including you.

- DOUBT

  - What potential doubt has!

  - Doubt accompanies us constantly. We keep planning the future, not knowing if we'll be living 'till the next day. But even our own past, carried in knapsacks of memories sometimes seems incredible, such is the jumble within.

- DREAM

  - It is possible that even babies dream dreams. They prattle, make sounds; they even smile with their eyes closed—at a time when they seem to be incommunicado with people around them.

E

- ELEGANCE

  – The superlative test of elegance is passed when you have to live in extreme poverty.

- EMBARRASSMENT

  – Repeated or extended embarrassment is only apparently "easy to take". It accumulates, in fact, and this leads towards separation, which is created by gradual distancing. Just when one was under the impression that … it disappeared naturally.

- EMPATHY

  – Empathy: an illusion. We are aiming at it, but we cannot reach it, no matter how much we would like to "put ourselves in the place of the other one". This does not excuse us from trying to take part in someone's troubles.

- ENAMORED

  – How beautiful are enamored people!

  – The laws of good cohabitation are necessary for everyone—including the enamored, so that they become one.

- ENEMY

    - Our enemies do not mark us less than our friends.

- ENVY

    - We would never envy anyone if we would be aware we are all living through good and bad times in amounts that only each of us can personally assess. We take turns, however, with our lives, and today one of us is laughing, and the other is crying, tomorrow things will be the other way around, and everything keeps repeating all the time, with gaps in time, with a lot of suffering, in such unbelievable, unknown degrees of pain.

    - Envy: admiration, negatively framed.

- EQUAL

    - In continually searching for our equals, we keep encountering people who are either below or above us. This leads to delayed harmony or the loss of any chance for certain harmonious relations.

- EQUILIBRIUM

    - The instability of the equilibrium between mind and soul makes for variations, movements, changes. It gives new meaning to each moment. That said, it does not necessarily make for happiness.

- EVENT

    - Why do we want special events to happen every day?

- EXASPERATION

  - It is exasperating when the weather is so beautiful and everyone wants you to be in tune with the nature, to exalt, to sing along with the birds, to bloom with the flowers, under a big blue sky – trying to turn you serene like it. And, in fact, you are an ocean of tears.

- EXPECTATION

  - Expectations are based on optimism.

F

- FACE

  - There is never so much light radiating from someone's face than at the mention of their beloved's name.

- FAITH

  - To have faith, to believe in God means not only to have no doubts about His existence, but also to do everything the way we understand His will. For everybody, this means to live a fully human existence.

- FASHION

  - Fashion forces you to compare what is trendy to what becomes you. Maybe you are lucky enough to live at a time which favors your physical being. You can also live at a time when your features and coloring are at odds with fashion. The only solution is good taste—unperturbed by the caprices of the provisional present.

  - In almost all fashions, new trends first become usual, then common, then out-of-date. Old trends come back and make a revival. It pays to be careful!

- FAULT

    - Minor flaws – always difficult to be detected, more difficult to be exposed. Fundamental faults – almost impossible to conceal forever. They are, however, committed by people (if they still qualify for this name) who reach the point of believing in the "truth" of their actions, functioning in a climate where horror is just normal.

- FEAR

    - Fear stops affecting you when you have lost everything. In a life whose main reason was love, blessed love, what can scare you after death has robbed you of the love of your life? What else remains to be taken from you, so that you should be afraid of a loss?

    - Fear of making mistakes can be paralyzing. Therefore, the more we accept to be afraid, the more lives become incomplete.

    - The greatest fear unites all fear—one that existed before us and in anticipation of things we don't yet know— even when realizing that they will hurt. What a terrible sum that incorporates memory and imagination!

    - Fear and hatred are often bedmates.

- FEEL

  - Why can we not order ourselves to feel the way we know it would be good for us?

- FEELING

  - Feelings for other people which are not reciprocated at their same level of quality represent useless waste.

- FLAW

  - Knowing the flaws and the weak spots of the others helps shortening the way of mutual understanding.

- FORGIVENESS

  - Between us and forgiveness there is always memory. The idea I (should) forgive, but I (should) forget not. Reference source: "(Our Father who are in Heaven) forgive us our trespasses as we forgive those who trespass against us." Do we really wish to be forgiven (only) in as much as we (generally) forgive those who have hurt us? How many times in life do we reach this summit of forgiveness? And how many times we ought to?

  - Both at confession and when we make "confidences" we hope to receive consolation and forgiveness, in return.

  - At best we offer partial forgiveness to others, while we expect total forgiveness from them.

- FRIEND

  - Real friends—and only real ones—can correctly appreciate the difference between discretion and absence.

  - There is an enormous distance between so called "former friends" – those people from whom life has separated us – and "former friends" – people from whom we tore ourselves away. The first category is made of friends whom we lovingly include in our nostalgia, where as the other ones are erased from our memory, while we are also likely to wonder whether we have ever been associated with them.

  - "True friend" is a pleonasm, which we learn to tolerate. How can a friend be other than true, totally true?

  - Your friend is your only equal.

  - A friend is a person who intuits when you are in need—one who does not have to wait for neither suggestions nor invitations to help you. By contrast, other people do.

- FRIENDSHIP

  - We must protect our long lasting friendships, since we will never be able to say: now I'll create an old friend for myself!

  - Friendships which seem very promising from a distance become, when living close to one another, less important, or even stop being friendships. As we know this risk, why are we still tempted to try closeness?

– An "identical" friendship can never be repeated.

• FUTURE

– An intrinsic element of the future are suppositions.

G

- GENEROSITY

  - Generosity implies sacrifice—not just renunciation …

- GOD

  - How would our lives be if we were spending every day, yes absolutely every day under the sign of "nihil sine Deo"?

  - God—to Whom each religion ascribes different names, different theologies—hears and understands prayer in all-world languages.

  - We call-out to God all the time. We look for Him in all things … He is next to us—in that person beside us, who also is looking for God …

  - We cannot "feel" God … neither can we describe Him … nor can we touch Him. We strive to prove His inexistence as the very least.

- GOOD

  - It is easy to think of yourself as good—as long as you are not put into a situation where you actually have to choose between good and evil.

- GOOD DEED

  - Ignoring a good deed is very much alike to doing a bad one.

- GRATITUDE

  - Gratitude can rebuild the equilibrium in many relationships which seem to be—otherwise—without solution.

  - To wonderful friends who have helped me throughout my life, I am always wishing to never need me to repay their kindness. Never. Despite the fact that I would do it form the bottom of my heart, and satisfied to be able to restore at least minimally the scales of fairness between giving – to receive – and repaying with great gratitude.

- GREED

  - Greed is a vice. Even though it is not obvious, greed is well related to stinginess. While the greedy man keeps hoarding things with avidity, and the avaricious one does not give away anything of his stock piles, they gather together, under the same roof. Generosity was banished from that place long before.

  - Greed removes boundaries between need and appetite.

H

- HABIT

  - Habits are acquired through patience and lost with difficulty. Sometimes, their loss creates suffering—not predicted while we were striving to develop them.

- HAPPY

  - Happy people cannot do evil things, therefore those who do evil things, either by words or by their actions – are (also) getting (some of) our compassion.

- HARMONY

  - To find the way which leads us to harmony, we should be able to reconcile what we are thinking with what we are saying, and with what we are doing.

  - We should avoid both those people who are always criticizing us and those who are praising us too much. Both praising and criticism, used excessively, upset the scales of harmony.

- HATE (HATRED)

  - A good key to the gates of hell: hate.

- And yet: where does one gather so much energy for hating, despite knowing that hate poisons us?

- How much hatred can germinate within pain—exploding with unexpected power? How long can it last?

- A strong sentiment—hatred—could it be a disease? Is it caused by something which we cannot understand—much less share?

- HAVE

  - All our belongings have us, in different proportions, but unavoidably.

- HELP

  - When helped, we should not assume that sacrifices would necessarily follow.

  - We should not appreciate our friends by the amount of help they gave us, but by what we suppose they were able to do for us.

- HIDING PLACE

  - There is no perfect hiding place where we can escape for good. If it existed or if it could even be invented, who would not live somewhere that forever holds reality at bay?

- HOLIDAY

  - The eve of a holiday is full of anticipation and charms you with sublimated joy.

- HOPE

  - "Still yes", "not yet": do these symbolize hope?

  - As oppressive as uncertainty is, it still allows to save a little corner for hope. A hope to which we are clinging at all costs, preferring to ignore real probabilities (some of which are terrifying).

I

- IF

  - The question *What if?* is so seductive by virtue of the many options it proffers, but it is also distressing for all the possibilities which depend upon it.

- IGNORE

  - Being "misunderstood" is based on "ignoring". Having an unrefined attention, we are absently passing by very significant things, getting just a glimpse of them, without absorbing them consciously and, evidently, without ever cogitating about their meaning.

- ILLUSION

  - Illusions are interesting, memories are boring.

  - How long can an illusion last?

  - We love our illusions!

  - Illusions are a kind of stubborn hope.

- IMAGINATION

  - How much imagination would we need to make us able to stop imagining?

- IMPATIENCE

    - Impatience interposes (itself) between us and the peace due to the order of things. How much calm we could gain if we only understood that "For everything there is an appointed time, even a time for everything under the heavens." (Eccl. 3:1)

- IMPORTANT

    - The very "important" things: <u>the</u> ours! You are irritated by a simple scratch, and you are worried by a little cold, generally, if they are yours. And you are more upset by them and certainly at least more immediately upset than by a serious and dangerous disease of a neighbor, an acquaintance, or of so many other people.

    - How much of what we perceive as very important at a given moment remains as such when we reevaluate everything, when the end comes?

    - The most important man in my life can only be the one I love best. To some, he must be the most powerful ... still for others, the most useful.

- INCOMPLETE

    - All things already in existence are incomplete.

- INDECISIVENESS

  - To justify our indecisiveness we know how to quote the fluid couple "on the one hand, on the other hand".

- INDIFFERENCE

  - The difficulty of expressing your indifference towards somebody comes from the necessity to demonstrate in a very convincing way the existence of " …something unexisting".

- INSULT

  - Some "guffs" are actually insults in disguise.

  - Instead of censoring themselves, rude people portray their insults as acts of sincerity.

  - We can insult people in well chosen, extremely refined words. We can console people with very simple, ordinary, not at all special words. Because the art of dealing with words is always conditioned by: the tone sets the music.

- INTELLIGENT

  - How much you can be isolated by being too intelligent!

- INTERESTING

  - Not all things that appear to be interesting now will stand the test of time and become important.

- INTIMACY

  - Without respect, intimacy degrades—simply and starkly—into closeness. Partners can end-up tolerating each other unconditionally and out of habit.

- ISOLATION

  - With greater isolation we deem ourselves more "original."

J

- JOY

  - How could we doubt the implicit joy coming from good deeds? Their discretion is answered, commensurate with their value, the divine reward. ("Your Father who is looking on in secret will repay you". Matthew 6:4)

K

- KEEP QUIET

  - You keep quiet for being ignorant, or because you are powerlessly afraid, because of indolence, or since you doubt the power of your voice could change something. You keep quiet, being afraid that you'll make yourself sound ridiculous.

  - We talk, we function, we dream … and we keep quiet in our own language.

- KISS

  - A kiss can replace worlds of words. It can also lie …

- KNOW

  - A person can be admired--even loved--by some, while despised--even hated--by others. The same person can look straight into our eyes or completely avoid looking at us. Still, we mirror her/him. We believe that we have deciphered her/him exactly as she/he is. We hope that we know this person. We hope that this person is real--one whom we see on all accounts. At the same time, this same person is reflected in no one.

  - To know, to realize, to understand the world. Children don't know how to do it, yet, or know very little. Old people don't know any more, or know very little. The rest of us already went through experiences the children had, so that we can laugh at their acts of foolishness. But how could we laugh at the old people, now reversing to "children's minds", the unknown world we had never stepped in so far, and which we fear increasingly, as we are getting closer to it?

L

- LANGUAGE

  - Both truth and lies need the almighty weapon of language.

  - In extreme situations, language offers the simple solution of "yes" or "no." A couple of syllables can quickly change someone's fate forever.

  - FOREIGN LANGUAGE

    - Small confusions can cause big troubles. The person who has to navigate in a second language knows well why she/he terms it—with a bit of "dis-ease"—a "foreign language."

  - MOTHER LANGUAGE (MOTHER TONGUE)

    - It is tempting to characterize languages as "beautiful" or "ugly." Maybe this happens by comparing collections of sound provided by nature? Maybe the perfect harmony of music plays into this? How much more emotion figures into this assessment when the message is delivered in your mother tongue.

- LAUGH

  - At the very least it is indecent to laugh when others are crying. Even though we know that life is offering both the crying and the laughter, to each of us, but in turn, and not at the same time.

  - How can we laugh at the nose of the clown?

- LAZINESS

  - Laziness: a form of powerlessness. Can a lazy person surpass him/herself? Does he/she want it? Does he/she understand the limits of his/her performance and indulges in it?

- LAZY

  - Lazy people know well how to procrastinate.

- LEARN

  - I have not met many people from whom I learned nothing at all.

- LIE

  - Convincing lies can become even more dangerous for their authors, the liars.

  - Lying is both a cause of and an effect of evil.

  - Lies represent yet another miserable face of powerlessness.

- We remember better the lies to which we were subjected--better than those we told. We need to continually feed those of our own creation--or risk exposure.

- After a lie, a complete lie, a partial lie, an occasional lie, an explained lie … even an "innocent" lie, nothing absolute can ever follow.

- A convincing lie may be most dangerous to its author—the liar.

- LIFE

  - It takes so very little for the whole course of your life to change!

  - Life is the inseparable combination between events and perceptions.

  - It is useless to try to learn all the "rules of the game" of life. They keep piling up in front of you, until you reach the end of your life.

  - Life, in short: we all (are sure that we already) have a past; not all of us (can be sure that we still) have a future!

- LIGHT

  - We yearn for light, but its brightness can blind us.

  - For as long as we live, let us save a spark of light—even when darkness tries is snuff it out. Light is created of light.

- LIMIT

  - Both advances and halting are conditioned by limits. Why does it not occur to us that we can also establish improved standards based on "when," "where," "how," and especially "why?"

- LISTEN

  - Being deaf: either because you cannot hear, or because you don't (know how to) listen? Almost curable or remediable – in the first case, very difficult to fix in the second.

- LIVE

  - We live, see, we live. Because we hope, justified or not, either confronting disaster (quite seldom) or taking refuge in denial (quite often); lying to ourselves. And, maybe, mixing curiosity about what is still lying in our future – our curiosity being a mobilizing ingredient in this process. The fact is, we are living!

- LONELINESS

  - We can live with loneliness – as ghastly as this thing is – for as long we know that somewhere somebody is still waiting for us. For as long as we know that somebody is still wondering what is happening with us, as long as somebody is aware that we are sharing the same universe, as long as somebody cares deeply if we are still alive. And that somebody cares deeply enough to check on us at least occasionally.

- The loneliness which terrifies us does not accept "degrees" of compassion, since it exists as an absolute.

- How much loneliness can we <u>put up</u> with?

- You do not possess loneliness; it possesses you.

- Caught in a crevice, you discover loneliness while among friends—both filled with them and inhabited by nobody. We kneel as if reiterating the prayer in Gethsemane--with tears addressed to God, the Heavenly Father. Meanwhile, the apostles sleep a tranquil and ignorant sleep (Matthew 14:36). Absolute quiet—then as now—in a harrowing void.

- LONGING

  - Longing: it allows no comparison, it has no limits, it cannot be cured.

- The death of your lover fills your loneliness with a LONGING that can never be cured.

  - Real longing means hurting.

- LOSE

  - Can we ever lose a thing without even a little regret?

- LOVE

  - In an existence built on the sacred elements of faith, hope, and love, "the greatest of these is love" (Paul, Cor. 1:13). And love alone is multiplying while one is sharing it.

  - We cannot decide either upon our birth, nor upon our death (exception: successful suicides!). But it is in our power to chose love, which is not less bright than a birth, being like a renewal, and stronger than death, whom it can outlive.

  - Even death cannot kill an immortal love!

  - Love which is not reciprocated does not deserve the sublime name of "love".

  - Fulfilled love should always make us all the more generous.

  - Dream and reality only commingle in love.

  - Is there any bigger poverty than being unable to love?

  - When you discover that a person you have loved is not the way you had imagined him/her, you realize that you have loved somebody who does not exist in reality. Despite the wasted time, everything gets unraveled, but you must have the will to admit your error … and the sooner, the better.

- Love is the chance to have met you. Luck is that you met me ... Luck is that we met each other ... It is the joy of sharing the gift of memories. Pain comes with having **only** memories ...

- What sense is there in asking true love to be "real"? Asking passion to be moderate?

- What remains meaningful is that which follows the lovers' encounter--after the physical act of love is consummated. It is preceded by an infinity of promises caused by attraction.

- Real love means: I am you; you are me. It does not mean: You are mine; I am yours.

- We often forget little amorous acts. We never forget the crazy acts of love.

- What an immense loss for mankind is the love which never finds its own voice.

- No pure thought, no embrace, nothing shared is ever lost. All love is gathered somewhere—morphing into a cosmic treasure and returning ceaselessly. It remains with us, with others, for us, for others, a gift manifested and countless ...

- Eternally strong, love reciprocating rejuvenates ... Only ignored love wilts us.

- There is no impossible love--even if the price is sometimes frightful.

- It takes two people for an act of love: you love somebody; that person loves you. Otherwise, it is a matter of fixation, obsession, fiction.

- There exists only one person in your life to whom you can say: I loved you even before I met you. It was not a mistake waiting for you all this time ...

- Can two people love each other equally? Are there differences in the ways of love—or only in its intensity? Is there a standard for this singular gift in life?

M

- MANKIND (MAN; PEOPLE)

  - Neither good things, nor bad things are due to "those people", but to "us, people".

  - We have "principles" and knowledge about the world, about people-in-general. But we get stuck as soon as we have to apply them in dealing with a single individual.

  - The world is full of good people getting bad advice.

  - Meetings with good people: celebrations!

  - If we could only love people unconditionally— without wondering how much love each one deserves ...

  - We must navigate between people who exasperate us with platitudes and those who overwhelm us with surprises.

  - Your life consists of people playing a significant role, people occupying a definitive role, and ... "others."

  - There are two categories of people: persons and characters.

  - I have never met a person without merit. I have never met a person without any flaw. In those with many qualities, I always thought even more positive qualities could be detected. In those with many flaws, I suspected even more flaws existed. In time, my "assumptions" were confirmed in both directions. Would this be a realistic assessment of people's characters, or is it rather a thing based on personal affinities?

- MEMORY

  - We are the synthesis of our memories. Without them, we do not recognize ourselves.

  - Nothing can replace common memories.

  - We live without being aware that we continue to create memories, which are the fabric of life. Some of them will outlive us.

  - The moment in which we can no longer plan for the future coincides—sadly too often—with the moment when there is no longer anyone with whom to share memories.

  - The memory of the first "I love you" and of the last "good bye" morph into "Adieu!" They will always remain with you in the language in which you first heard them.

  - Memories, a consolation?

  - We cannot select our memories, and this is yet another case when we are powerless.

- Without memories we would be living in chaos. They are both levers in the world we are populating, and gates for nostalgia.

- Common memories are an essential ingredient of friendships.

• MESSENGER

- A messenger is as important as the message itself—even if a messenger—by tradition—is seen as neutral.

• MIDDLE GROUND

- "Middle ground" is seldom placed in the middle of the road.

• MIRROR

- Mirrors separate time from space. They render an image at the moment of reflection, and you no longer exist in them once you turn your back.

- Mirrors are merciless witnesses and convey the verdict of time.

• MISTAKE

- We must avoid both mistakes and sins, even though we hope we will be judged more lightly for our mistakes than for our sins.

- Explanations, justifications, reasons, motives, even regrets, cannot totally excuse various mistakes due to no matter what causes. But how much we hope they could do this!

– There is an unremovable barrier between fixing a mistake and annulling it.

– In what void should you be living so that you never make mistakes?

– Our mistakes should make us more tolerant of another's mistakes. They should make us more conscientious that imperfections complete imagined perfection.

– Are we making a mistake in trying to define mistakes? A wrong thing … compared to what?

• MOMENT

– As in Goethe's Dr. Faust's prayer, the absolute moment has to stop. Since we do not know how to stop time, we are caught lusting after it in a kind of miracle-fantasy. An individual moment cannot last forever, and it will never come back. Some other moments—all too ordinary—push back further and further and down so rapidly and without any memory.

• MOTHER

– We applaud, appreciate, respect the author of ten books, the composer of ten musical compositions, the painter of ten paintings, the sculptor of ten statues, etc. But we know next to nothing about so many mothers of ten great children each, at most we know that such mothers exist …

– How wonderful is the dialogue between mother and child—a unique act of communication and based on only a few sounds for a whole world of meanings.

• MUSIC

– Nothing can be more eloquent than music.

– A blessing for somebody you love: May you always be alive in music!

• MYSTERY

– We are all mysteries for each other.

– We are always attracted to mysteries; we look for them. By contrast, things natural or banal or trivial are easily predicted in daily activities. We do not pursue them with passion; we do not risk for them.

N

- NEVER

  - "Never" almost perfectly mates with "impossible"—separating us from everything possible and to no avail. Surprisingly, it will happen anyway.

- NIGHT

  - Night is when you best understand loneliness.

- NIGHTMARE

  - Why does the superlative of evil—suffering, fear, despair (all real states)--why does it always result in nightmares? We fear the loss of control, and weakness plays out in bad dreams.

- NOSTALGIA

  - The deepest nostalgia: longing for ourselves. We project this feeling against times and places, against people and situations, accepting even our sufferings from passed times, in our melancholy, as these sufferings are also a part of ourselves.

- NOTABLE POINT

  - The first time ... the first mistake ... the first quarrel between lovers. The first car accident. The first disappointment in a friendship. The first big loss. Without these notable points we cannot be in love, disappointed, harmed, shocked. We just cannot be! The first time is the beginning—one that cannot be repeated.

- NUANCE

    - Nuances: in every relation, they are what brings us closer, and they are what distances us, as well.

    - "Grey" is an attractive nuance because it sits between "white" and "black." If we reduce everything to "pure" grey, we no longer see intermediary shades, no differing degrees. Then if we add a color, we lose the subtlety provided only by nuance. This is proof of the universal and indefinite palette!

- NUMBNESS

    - The inability to forget pain forces you towards a prayer for eternal numbness.

0

- OBJECT

    - Why do objects have such power over us? Because we consume ourselves in seeking them out and acquiring them. Later we care for them, maintain them, preserve them. Once they are integrated into our universe, we unconsciously associate them with significant moments, with remarkable people in our lives. Finally, objects turn into symbols.

- OBLIVION

    - Blessed oblivion: the moment that crowns forgiveness.

    - Oblivion keeps us from insanity.

    - We "understand" horrible things so as to liberate ourselves—almost to the point of oblivion. Total understanding is difficult—maybe even inconceivable. When we do not want to identify with the authors of extreme evil—the "great" criminals—we dream of oblivion. Such a summit of nobility is nearly unattainable.

    - Oblivion is fueled by indifference.

- OBSESSION

  - There is no place for reasoning in obsession. Obsessions do not fit the rules. They are not open to argument. They never tire. They merely exist.

- OLD AGE

  - Everyone ages differently—or, at least, tries to do so. What a shocking equalizer old age is.

  - The older you get, the more witness to your youth is lost. You sometimes get lost, and you look for guidance in mirrors and in echoes. Your shadow keeps you company, and it follows you to a point. Then comes old age, and total amnesia sets in.

  - Old age requires more self control than the years which precede it, therefore we must resist as long as we can. What is ridiculous for young people becomes pathetic in old age, and things which are disgusting about young people can be repulsive – why indeed? – in old people. Careful, therefore, about odd clothing, about foul language, and about gestures which are out of place. And we don't need to interpret "the golden years" as a … new youth, as an absolute truth. We are always aiming at terrific performances, but it is terrible when the swan song at the end of our life misses dignity: the supreme legacy.

- OLD PEOPLE

    - Old people's memories: their treasure and their burden, their agony.

    - Older people try to fill the present emptiness with memories and imagination. It is all illusion.

    - Todays' old people are yesterday's youth; today's youth will be tomorrow's old people. All that changes is the incidental of time.

    - Because they so want to be "accepted," old people often project themselves as young in body and in soul. They even try to find "research" to argue this. What good is it? Another and unchangeable reality draws close …

- OPINION

    - We represent the sum total of others' opinion about and opinions of us. How much they admire, value, and love us … How much they dislike, detest, despise us. Opinions can be right or wrong, but how much room is left to doubtful assessments?

    - We have the right to change our opinions—just not our promises. How closely intertwined they often are!

- OPTIMISM

  - We do not base our hopes on optimism. However, we do need hope to bridge the connection to the next moment.

- ORIGINAL

  - Even when we connect with others with whom we have enough in common, we are tempted to go our separate way—since the desire to be "original" is so strong.

- ORIGINALITY

  - True originality stands apart from both banality and terribleness. A real connoisseur recognizes it with no effort. An ignorant man often gets confused.

P

- PASSION

    - Passion is not learned.

    - Passion is a thirst not quenched with water; it dies by devouring itself.

- PAST

    - The past is expanding as much as the future is abbreviated, until, quite shocked, we are reduced to saying that the future is now! And even then, we are still hoping that we are a little bit wrong when assessing time ...

- PATIENCE

    - Patience is a virtue much underrated by those who confuse it with placidity.

    - Patience is measured against time, which seems infinite.

- PLACIDITY

    - Placidity, without a proper dose, is the opposite both of too much worry and of blessed serenity.

    - Placidity is inborn, but patience requires effort.

- PLANS

  - We like to listen to ourselves making big plans, while (so called) small things are eroding our foundation.

- PLAY

  - Games are fun until the temptation to play with fire becomes part of the game, which always changes the rules of the game.

- POLYGLOT

  - We do not sufficiently appreciate polyglots. We do not recognize their role in breaking down barriers— an indispensable act to promote understanding each other.

- POWER

  - Ah, power is full of venom!

  - Our power rests on all the mistakes we have made— from which we were able to learn.

- PRAY

  - There exists no language in which one cannot pray quietly, aloud, alone, or together with others.

- PRAYER

  - In a worst-case scenario prayer helps you understand that you are not the "center" of the universe, that not everything depends upon you. Rather it allows you to be protected, to be enveloped in hope.

– We base all our prayers on "Thy will be done" from Our Lord's Prayer realizing that God knows, in absolute, what is best for us. Time keeps confirming our trust.

– Following the way time is structured, we are planning our lives in agreement with calendars and clocks. Only prayers cannot be forced with a corset if we are living according to the wonderful teachings of St. Paul's: "Pray incessantly." (1 Test. 5:1)

– Among the terrible sufferings of our Savior—the night of His loneliness in Ghetsemane. There is no other way to emerge from darkness, but by the solitary prayer, pained, but steady, the prayer we are relying on through times.

• PREDESTINATE

– It is hard to argue that someone will likely die in a crash on a plane other than the one predestined for him. That ticket for her/his last trip was reserved long ago ...

• PREFER

– Some people prefer to be loved, some others – to be admired, others to be well paid. And, twisted around an unnatural axis, there are those who want to be feared, living with the illusion of becoming omnipotent.

- I am the involuntary witness of a piece of a dialogue: "would you prefer to be blind or to be deaf?"

- **PRESENT**

  - The present time is our compromise between things we can no longer have and those we do not yet possess—between melancholy and aspirations.

  - Missed moments can never be replaced by "other" moments. The present knows no "other time."

  - While we are trying to size-up the moment, to live in the moment, to consume it—that moment has already gone forever. What only remains is the conventional notion of "between the past and the future."

- **PRIDE**

  - Which is the relation between pride and courage?

  - Pride of a dignified kind is separated from conceitful pride by an abyss—not by steps.

- **PRINCIPLE**

  - Strict principles lead us blindly. They replace inspiration—precluding understanding a different point-of-view.

- **PROJECT**

  - How eloquent are the newly started projects left "unfinished"—abandoned by someone's death.

- PROMISE

  - Promises fulfilled: words made flesh. Otherwise, just empty words …

  - Many promises are made with the intention to anesthetize.

  - One needs to correctly understand the value of a promise.

- PROUD

  - Earning the right to be proud, we can become modest.

  - To be proud? To be strong (as well)?

  - A great victory of a proud person is to learn when to apologize, whether it is certainly necessary to do so, but even when it is only probably needed.

- PUNISHMENT

  - Are there any punishments which are completely devoided of the sense of revenge?

Q

- QUESTION

    – Something is wrong at the point when there are no questions left.

    – Opinions and suggestions in delicate questions are priceless. They are completely different from interrogations—which only indicate curiosity.

    – The question of all questions: Which question would you like never to be posed?

- QUIETUDE

    – Rare are the places for quiet: nighttime, a church, a mountain, a cemetery, an embrace, a whisper, music/music/music, and caressing …

    – A dictionary of quietude?

R

- RAPE

    - Emotional rape can be more damaging than physical rape. It can be so brutal as to preclude even involuntary climax.

- REACTION

    - For identical reasons, some people are doing so much good, and others – so much evil. Which, of course, makes us wish to be able "to explain" their why-so-s, seeing their completely opposite reactions.

- RELATIONSHIP

    - Human relationships do not exist "in general." Relationships are between you and me, between him and her, between us and you, etc. Neither do they exist in the time-frame called "forever." Relationships predominantly happen in the "now," the "then," the "here," the "there," in "another time" …

    - We assess people depending on our relationship to them, although we like to believe that we view them objectively.

    - Which is the best thing, and which is the worst thing we can say about our closest friends? And which are the best and the worst things we can say about our most insufferable enemies? And how does our relationship with these people define us?

- REMORSE

  - Remorse: superlative case of regrets, applied to first person singular.

- RENUNCIATION

  - Not all renunciations are victorious.

  - Renunciation? Defeat? If we only could avoid defeats, knowing how to say "no" while there is still time for doing so.

- REPETITION

  - A beautiful *leitmotif* accompanies you, enchants you, charms you … A banal repetition follows you and exasperates you.

- REPLACE

  - Do not forget that there is no irreplaceable object-- while not one single human being can be replaced.

- REPROACH

  - Either reproaches, or sadness, they seldom speak in the same voice.

  - Reproaches: regrets, of different degrees, which are voiced. And sometimes, in a very clumsy way.

- RESIGNATION

  - How much resignation is part of tolerance?

- RESPONSIBILITY

  - We are really the synthesis of everything we achieved or that we tried to achieve—either in building or in destroying. We always carry an element of responsibility.

- REVENGE

  - Revenge allows the impression of "reward," which is a really toxic poison. Its effect passes in a moment.

- RISE

  - Yes! Rise gently! Rise like an arrow—higher and higher to your summit in the sky! Never accept a pedestal—one constructed of human lives.

- RISK

  - What a great number of chances are ruined by the fear of risking!

- ROUTINE

  - A miserable substitute for enthusiasm, routine helps us crawl ahead when we cannot soar.

- RUSHING

  - Rushing ... the enemy of taking a break. Short breaks, in praise of speed, shorter nights, breaking apart borders among colors, rhythmic contractions in … inspiration, breathing, silence … replacing everything with access and availability to everything. Acquiring information … increased production. In short, it is the creation of a continuum from an old dream—a creation that now controls you.

S

- SACRIFICE

  - What remains from a useless sacrifice other than defeat?

- SEASONS

  - Seasons … Why does autumn come more quickly than springtime?

- SECRET

  - Why does one have secrets? Because of modesty, or is it because of being cautious?

- SEEM

  - We cannot be objective—maybe not even strong. Joys are too fleeting, while suffering seems to drag on …

- SELF-DEFINE

  - How would you define yourself in a single word in your own sweet, rich, native language? How would others define you? The "image-word" is priceless because it is both a memory and a promise at the same time. The greatest word is your word-of-honor (parole d'honeur) while the words chiseled into your gravestone will mark you forever.

- SELF-LOVE

  - How sterile is self-love!

- SELF-PORTRAIT

  - In characterizing other people you often paint yourself much better than you would in a self-portrait.

- SELFISHNESS

  - Selfishness does not protect you from others. Rather it unravels you—fiber by fiber. At first the fraying is invisible … ultimately, it rips you completely apart.

- SENSE

  - We need the senses that are always cited, sight, hearing, smell, taste, touching. But how could we live adequately without a sense of humor and the sense of the ridiculous?

- SENTIMENTALIST

  - The sentimentalist is not always an altruistic person.

- SEPARATION

  - There is a sadness unique to people in love, who have recently separated—a sadness seen on their faces and nowhere else.

- Nobility can make separation more difficult to bear than a bit of meanness—which could act out of charity by sparing us idealized memories.

- After a separation, each day starts with mantras like "first-day-without-you," "second-day-without-you," "third-day-without-you" … followed by "the-days-without-you" … "all-the-days-without-you."

- Some separations maim us.

- In a separation described as "mutual consent" somebody leaves first, however. Should we admire that person, for having a clear perspective? Or blame him/her for impatience?

- Separations: essential element in our life, into which we are running again and again. It culminates with death, for which nothing can "prepare" us enough …

- Why is the moment of separation lagging in us for so long?

• SHAME

- The ugly world begins where shame ends.

• SILENCE

- How big is the chasm between "quiet" and "silence!"

- Words bear repeating, but every silence is different. We can frequently render words exactly, but we can never render silence.

- SIN

  - The greatest sin is to cause suffering--ignoring it in others.

- SLEEP

  - Dreams surpass our illusions and nightmare surpasses our biggest fears. Their common territory is sleep. Is this the bridge between life and death?

  - Sleeplessness: due to our fear of nightmares; nightmares: due to our being exhausted by sleeplessness. We are looking for a refuge: to be found in the prayer: "Deliver us from evil" …

- SPACE

  - If the real universe does not accommodate you, create a beautiful and parallel world of your own—your own space, a place of refuge.

  - The gilded cage: the castle which separates you from the rest of the world—a space to lock yourself up—willingly and, still, hopefully.

  - Your space: a nest, a burrow, a citadel—or a prison?

- SPHINX

  - You need a sphinx to confront another sphinx.

- STUBBORN

    - Nobody seems more stubborn than the one who disagrees with you.

- STUBBORNNESS

    - Stubbornness is a monolith. We cannot penetrate it. On occasion (and with diplomacy), we can cheat it.

    - Stubbornness: a proof of "will power" of weak people.

- SUFFER

    - There are two distinct species: those who have already suffered profoundly and those who haven't yet.

- SUFFERING

    - Beware of taking suffering lightly! Remember that each time you hurt someone, the suffering lasts all day—minute by minute, day and night, never coming nor going. Always remember everything that has hurt you in life!

    - It is insane to try to speak about suffering. Pain screams, howls, explodes, burns, consumes. Pain destroys the mind. Ultimately, no words can describe pain.

    - We cannot judge--nor measure--suffering. We can barely understand another's wounds. Even when we draw close to them, we explore what lies beneath the surface. If we get inspired, we to try comfort—while simply "groping in the dark." If we feel powerless, we walk away--puzzled, thinking that we are useless. Are we actually defending ourselves?

— Everything, yes, everything has an end. Why then, when suffering overwhelms us, do we not recall that suffering has no chance to last forever?

— Suffering: no matter how well you prepare for major pain, the reality exceeds all expectations.

— There is no suffering without "reason."

— We cannot learn to avoid suffering, despite all the "lessons" which are offered us. But we can learn how to behave when suffering.

— It is ridiculous to compare one suffering with another one, and it is in immense bad taste to try to establish the greatest of all sufferings.

— In the midst of pain we can not think of what is going to follow, what will follow does not exist at that point, and all we wish is the pain passes, for us to get rid of it, and, in the best possible scenario, we wish to be able to return to the way we have been before suffering started.

— Huge suffering never goes away. It is the mark of irreplaceable losses. But we hope that it will metamorphose and that we will be capable to survive. Eventhough to continue being implies our accepting the fact that it will be impossible to have a full life again.

- SUICIDE

  - Suicide is an answer. Still, those left behind also await an answer—those hanging on to the last note from the victim ... a small comfort and maybe an accusation.

  - Because suicide is a final act, nobody can tell us how things are afterwards. Thus, conflicting opinions regarding suicide—whether cowardice or courage—remain endlessly viable. Today you may be seated next to someone "philosophizing"–who, pushed to the limits, will commit suicide tomorrow.

  - Suicide is the final act of ... hope. The victim is trying to kill-off the unbearable pain in an attempt to get to a different place—to relocate to another dimension and to escape this unbearable one.

  - To the one who commits suicide, it is a cure for the disease that others call life.

  - The one who commits suicide is not trying to escape life—but rather to escape pain. For her/him, the present--the moment called "now"—is unbearable and has absolute value.

- SURPRISE

  - We enjoy just how far we reach with our creations, helped by modern technologies. At the same, time, we notice that the chances for surprise are diminished. Yes, we grow more powerful, but who or what is still able to surprise us?

- An extreme surprise: us, to ourselves, under the most unexpected circumstances.

- SUSPICIOUS

  - Many suspicious people like to be considered as cautious fellows.

T

- TABOO

  - We—each one of us—has another list of taboos.

- TALK

  - Talking at length is risky. We are boring those around us when we get started and seem to never end. Moreover, as we keep speaking, we get carried away, and we begin to add elements of little interest, and even maybe (relatively?) not true.

  - People are usually congratulating themselves for not talking about what they should not --(meaning) "silence is gold". There are, however, instances when you may feel awful for not having said things which might have been needed to be said as it was still time to have them said. This is an instance of the terrible "it is too late".

- TANGO

  - Tango is the dance of limitless promises.

- TEAR

  - Tears of the oysters – pearls. Our tears – words. Pearls – in all languages of the world. Words – in what language?

- TECHNOLOGY

  - New technologies really do enrich and empower us. They also tend to replace intimacy with indiscretion, which we have baptized, serenely, as "information."

  - What new technology can recreate the atmosphere of an intimate discussion between just two people? Is it possible that this kind of discussion is no longer desirable? Can you imagine that the emotional function of language will disappear completely?

- TELEPATHY

  - We cannot claim copyright for ideas transmitted by telepathy. But, sometimes, we would pay a great deal to be able to suggest, to attract, and to operate in the power of thinking.

- THANK YOU (THANKS)

  - "Thank you": a phrase whose meaning is either full of solemnity, or it only represents a banal formula. Repeated in our prayers, we expect it to be heard in its simplicity and splendor.

- THERAPIST

  - Various "therapists" can teach you how to function, but not how to live as well. Some of them have their answers = prescriptions, ready, even before hearing your questions.

- THINK

  - Talking the same language factually means thinking alike.

- THOUGHT

  - Which is the ugliest thought you have ever had?

- TIME

  - For the duration of our lives (the big unknown!) we are all fairly treated, by being installed from the start, in equal structures, named seconds, minutes, hours, days and nights, months, years. Some people, however like to describe themselves as "busier" (the magic word "busy"!), having less time, somehow implying … "more important"? Ignoring or neglecting the clock and the calendar, they don't notice the power priorities have. All of us are using quantitatively and/or qualitatively parts of what we were originally given. We are spending with our bodies, minds, and souls, we give and we take, and we perceive time either correctly or relatively so. But we can never get over the rigors of time – <u>usque ad finem</u>.

  - "Everything passes" does not represent the perfect equivalent of "Time heals all things." Scars are often ignored--especially the shadows and the echoes, the "memories-as-ghosts" forgotten.

  - How much time and struggle we waste in endless pursuit—by trying to rediscover a lost moment. We want to identify a trace--at least--a ghost that the moment had been real.

- Lovers are present too little; their absence too long. We never grow accustomed to time-irregularities.

• TOLERANCE

- Ignorance makes us involuntarily tolerant to intolerance.

- Tolerance can not be mistaken for indifference. Respect seems to be a good standard in discriminating between them.

• TRACE

- You should leave a trace in places through which you pass—at least a question, a souvenir, a shadow.

• TRUST

- What is the roadway that leads to trust? Our minds? Our souls? The intersection between them? A synthesis? An inspiration?

• TRUSTING

- An exceedingly trusting person needs—at least— one minimally suspicious friend.

• TRUTH

- Sometimes we look for truth—afraid of just what we may find!

- By reviewing the naked truth in all its unfiltered, spontaneous variants, we can censor self-expression—and loose what is most vivid in our thought-process.

- Truth has to battle with both ignorance and mistakes—as well as with lies and memory and "interpretations."

- Such a shame that skeptics' theories often include some kernel of truth.

- Precisely because it is elusive, "absolute" truth excites us to hunt it with such desperation.

- The truth is a victim when conflicts take place, either because of passion or in a calculated way.

- Short of having the truth, which is the worse answer? A lie or an "incomplete" answer? Neither is advisable. But sinful as we are, each of us tends to make different errors, according to our character.

• TRY

- We can always try ... just try.

U

- UNDERSTAND

    - When we do not understand something, we are tempted to say that it is untrue.

- UNDERSTANDING

    - We claim that we pursue understanding, while—in fact—we are seeking approval, support, and even applause.

    - Understanding is an absolute necessity for forgiveness, but, unfortunately, it is not a sufficient condition as well. We understand with our minds, we forgive with our souls. And then, in so many ways!

    - We must be very careful about the very fine line which separates "understanding" from "interpreting".

    - How much are we able to not understand? And to consider that we did understand – thus creating even more confusion – either because of being naïve, or because of arrogance?

    - Would we ever understand that there is no way to understand everything?

- UNHAPPINESS
  - Personal expectations for happiness are almost always unrealistic. It does not take much to consider ourselves unhappy.

V

- VICTIM

  - Only some victims are lucky enough to become heroes.

W

- WAIT

  - Ask the one who walks in front of you to wait for you. Accept the request of the one behind you to wait for him/her. You will become richer in both instances.

- WALTZ

  - You waltz because you dream of yourself in flight to the step of a waltz, flying …

- WAR

  - Why are we surprised that wars kill so many people? Still we go on elaborating on which means would be the best, how much suffering is acceptable from a humane point of view. Otherwise said, regarding at things from the point of view of life. But being at war means "to solve" conflicts through killing. Not through killing people as well, but just killing.

- WEAKNESS

  - It seems that shared weaknesses can bring us closer than shared merits do.

- WILL

  - A final will and testament is the last proof of love for someone. It connects the world of the living to that of the dead.

- WING

  - Once your wings are clipped, the ground does not recognize you—so you start to crawl.

- WISDOM

  - Intelligence and so much knowledge are shining. They attract, they charm. Depth can not be attained without wisdom, to which we are opening our heart in prayers ("Look! You have taken delight in truthfulness itself in the inward parts; and in the secret self may you cause me to know secret wisdom" Psalms 51:6).

- WOMAN

  - Women love either fiercely or with mercy. Their passion speaks with blood or tears. Hardly ever does a woman's love manifest itself in the raw act of sex.

- WONDER

  - The end is the moment when one no longer wonders about anything anymore.

- WORD

  - Words are never "just" words; they either always create sores or make a sweet-smelling balm.

  - Complicated words--uttered in the hope of connecting us better—are often "misunderstandable." They sound like indecipherable noises—misleading and dangerous. Too often, we simply forget the all-too-real lesson of Babel.

  - We put our biggest hopes in words—more than in any other thing. We always forget how treacherous words are.

- UGLY WORDS

  - We avoid impurities; we wash, filter, disinfect, and sterilize things. Yet, how well we tolerate vulgar, dirty, foul words—full of nasty messages from rude people—with all the filth that such people reflect and spread.

  - Parrots are so lucky! They remain attractive and amusing birds–no matter how many ugly words they caw. For the same performance, their mentors—people, those authors of dirty expressions—only gather contempt. —

A *Monologue on the Shores of the River of Life* is a collection of thoughts by Romanian-American author, <u>Alexandra Roceric</u>. They spring from simple musings--ones not easily classified thematically. They make no pretensions at being "ultimate truth." It is even difficult to categorize them as aphorisms, proverbs, or maxims. They might not even qualify as good advice in the classical sense! Simply put, they are propositions and questions; they are never spoken in jest.

After my husband's passing, thoughts were whirling around in the vacuum created by his absence. Yes, my sounding board was gone, but slowly some of these thoughts began to voice themselves. What had once been a dynamic dialogue morphed into a powerful monologue. Now in print, this *Monologue* just might elicit a response from some and even stimulate others.

Alexandra Roceric, Ph.D. is a Romanian-American philologist, who was educated and earned her PhD at the University of Bucharest, Romania. She was teaching/doing research at the Universities of Besançon (France), Prague (Czech Republic), Copenhague (Denmark), Lund (Sweden), Padova (Italy), and Stanford (USA).

Dr. Roceric emigrated to the United States in 1975, where she continued her scholarly work at the Catholic University of America (where she also earned a Master in Library and Information Science), Center for Applied Linguistics, and the Language Research Center, as well as at the Library of Congress, all in Washington DC.

She has authored six books in Linguistics (some in collaboration), and three volumes of poetry (bilingual editions). Her papers are included in volumes published in Austria, Canada, Denmark, France, Italy, Netherlands, New Zealand, Romania, and United States of America. Alexandra Roceric has extensively travelled in five continents. She has studied music (piano) – privately and in the Art School (Bucharest). And she volunteers in the medical support field (started in the Emergency Hospital in Bucharest, and then in a Free Clinic and currently in the Washington Home & Community Hospice of Washington DC). On a personal level, she considers these contributions of equal importance to her professional career, collaborations, accomplishments, and projects